PRESENTED TO

FROM

DATE

I WILL FOLLOW CHRIST

Clay Crosse   Bob Carlisle   BeBe Winans

J. COUNTRYMAN
Nashville, Tennessee

Published by J. Countryman®, a division of Thomas Nelson, Inc.,
Nashville, Tennessee 37214

I WILL FOLLOW CHRIST © 1999 Word Music, Inc.
Fifty States Music (Admin. By Word Music, Inc.)
Anything for the Kids Music (Admin. By Word Music, Inc.).
All Rights Reserved. Used by Permission.

Unless otherwise indicated, all Scripture quotations in this
book are from the New King James Version of the Bible (NKJV),
copyright © 1979, 1980, 1982, Thomas Nelson, Inc., Publishers.

J. Countryman® is a trademark of Thomas Nelson Inc.

Project editor: Jenny Baumgartner

Design: Koechel Peterson & Assoc., Inc., Minneapolis, Minnesota

Acknowledgement: "Compelled to Tell." Adapted from *Just Give Me
Jesus*, by Anne Graham Lotz. © 2000. Published by Word Publishing.

Photos on pages 7, 24, and 49 compliments of FreeStockPhotos.com

ISBN 0-8499-5745-1

Printed and bound in the United States of America

www.jcountryman.com

"Take up the cross, and follow Me."

MARK 10:21

The very beginning of an idea for the song "I Will Follow Christ" was revealed to me as I sat watching a Broadway musical. During the performance, a large chorus of men sang an intensely passionate song. They really put their hearts into it. I began to visualize the cast as the disciples, singing about their faith in Him. I knew immediately, "I must write a song about this." I contacted my friend, Steve Siler, to write the song with me.

Steve and I began to talk about the disciples and their time with Jesus. What an awesome experience that must have been for them: walking with Christ in the flesh, audibly hearing His words, seeing the miracles firsthand. What a great honor! Steve and I thought about how they must have felt when Jesus left them, when He ascended to heaven. Were they afraid? Were they joyous? Did they understand? Did they still believe? I'm sure they wrestled with and weighed all these things. The bottom line, though, is this: they kept following Him. They kept telling the world about Him. They served Him all the way to their deaths. Most importantly, they still believed and still followed Him.

As Steve and I began to think about ourselves and other modern-day believers, we set out to bridge the distance between the disciples' time and ours. Today, we've never walked with Jesus or lived with Him in the flesh. We don't know how His voice actually sounds. We don't know what He really looks like. But . . . WE STILL BELIEVE. He is in our lives. We can talk to Him, and He to us. Just like the disciples, we call Him "Father." Throughout the generations, He has touched lives. He has saved souls. He has been constant. That is the heart of "I Will Follow Christ." It's about knowing that He is real today and totally committing your life to Him.

I was blessed to have Bob Carlisle and BeBe Winans, as well as producer Regie Hamm, join me for the recording of this song. Their individual talents helped make the song special. My prayer is that this song will continue to be used by Him, for His glory. I want those who hear it to be encouraged so that they will give their daily lives to Him and will keep saying, "I Will Follow Christ!"

Clay Crosse [FALL 2000]

I Will Follow Christ [LYRICS]

The twelve of you walked on the earth together
The Father was a brother to you all
The teaching that you heard was the Living Word
The wonders and the miracles you saw

There were times of awesome inspiration
There were times you didn't understand
When He had to go and you felt alone
It must've been so hard to see His plan

I think about the way you carried on
In the face of persecution you stood strong

[CHORUS]

I will follow Christ
I will run the race
Fighting the good fight
Standing on my faith

I will wear the name of Jesus
I will give Him all my life
As for me no matter what the sacrifice
I will follow Christ

I don't have to look across the ages
His voice is speaking in my heart today
His Word is like a flame consuming all my shame
His life a shining star to show the way

[CHORUS]

I behold your life and see the man you want me to become
Living like someone who belongs to the kingdom
That was sealed on Calvary
I will show the world what I believe

[CHORUS]

 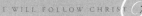

A New Longing for Christ

I am experiencing a new chapter in my life. Although I don't know the exact direction God is leading me, I do know that my heart is being prepared like never before. I feel that I have a better understanding of His heart.

There are several reasons for this understanding. One comes from parenting. My wife Jacque and I have raised one child to adulthood and are still parenting a teenager. In the process, I have felt emotions so strong that I can't help but compare them with how our Heavenly Father must feel about us. I can only imagine how passionate God is toward His children. Today, I better understand the words *unconditional, sacrifice, gratitude,* and *brokenness.*

I have also come to a better understanding of worship. It is a feeling of deep longing. As a father, would I rather hear my children say, "Dad, you are powerful and just, and you will forever be my only dad" or "Dad, I really want to be with you, because when I'm away, I miss you so much"? I'll take the latter anytime.

I am no longer satisfied with my prayer time where I stand before the throne and make requests. I long to pray like my wife, Jacque. She equates her "alone" time with God as that of a child. She just crawls up in His lap, puts her head against His chest, and listens to His heartbeat. My desire is to hear God's heartbeat.

Being a Christian for twenty-eight years does not give me spiritual seniority, but it has granted me a perspective that I could never have achieved earlier. I remember the times, even as a Christian, when I cursed, drank too much, hurt people, hurt myself, and worst of all, ignored and hurt God. But God did not ignore me. He pursued me, even when I didn't want to be pursued. He loved me when I was too drunk to drive home and when I got my nose broken in a parking lot brawl. Many times I didn't walk a straight path, but He kept me safe. I was still His kid. He still remembered the covenant I had made with Him, even when I refused to remember.

God is deeply concerned about me. He loves me and likes me, no matter what. That's the way I feel about my own kids. If my children were to ignore me, run from me, or tell me they didn't love me anymore, it would devastate me and break my heart, but I wouldn't refuse to be their dad. That's a covenant I made with them even while they were in the womb.

So now, as I enter this new chapter of my life, I'm not as concerned about what the future holds as I am about getting closer to Jesus. God has created this new longing in me because I surely didn't create it myself. It is with my realization of the past, my covenant with Him, and my new longing that I will continue to follow Christ . . . forever.

Bob Carlisle [CHRISTIAN ARTIST]

When your heart is full of Christ,

you want to sing.

CHARLES SPURGEON

Because He Loves Me

In my walk with Jesus, I have learned that He is the only fulfillment for my loneliness and my longing. I follow Him not just because of what He can give me but more because of the love He has shown me. To sum it up, I follow Christ because He really loves me.

Each day, I understand more that God is who He says He is. About four years ago, I learned about Jesus as Healer and Provider. He healed my brother Ronald after a near-fatal heart attack.

The doctors said that only 20 percent of Ronald's heart was still beating. My family and I were told to say our good-byes.

My mother asked us to pray as my brother went in for surgery. After the operation, the doctors said that Ronald had died on the table for five minutes, but they revived him. Only two days later, a sonogram showed that the right side of his heart—the side they said would never beat again—had started beating,

but the doctors were still doubtful. They told us that if Ronald got up and walked out of that hospital, then they would come to church.

Ronald's health continued to improve, and then on Easter Sunday morning, the doctors and nurses all came to church and testified about the miracle that took place with my brother's health.

God showed us that He heals, but as powerful as He is, He cannot move if there is doubt. We had two choices: we could take the facts route, or we could take the faith route. My family stood strong and chose faith, and I will never forget it.

I want to be and do more than I have ever done before for Christ. I want to display the love that God has shown me. That is why I am going to continue to follow Him, no matter what happens.

BeBe Winans [CHRISTIAN ARTIST]

An Eternal Love Affair

When I strip it all away—all of my life experiences, all of the influences, all of my efforts to be something, or even my desire to please others—when I get right down to finding out who I am, to discovering what's at the very core of me, the one thing that I know is that I am a child of God. In spite of this realization, I'm aware that my testimony isn't the most dramatic one out there, at least in comparison with some others I've heard, but I still know that my salvation is every bit as much a miracle. It's every bit as much a cause for celebration. I know that without Christ, I would be damned. Just as damned as anyone without Him in their life. With Him, though, I'm saved!

I was raised in a Christian home. To be able to say this, I realize that I'm in the minority in this world. Yes, I actually have parents who live what they believe. They always kept Christ as the center of our home. I'm eternally thankful for my upbringing. I came to accept Jesus as my savior when I was thirteen. I know that this decision was influenced greatly by what I had seen in my family. I knew, though, that my folk's faith alone wouldn't "get me to heaven." It wasn't enough. That's why I asked Him into my heart.

Now, as a grown man, a husband, and a father, it's interesting for me to look back through the years since that childhood decision. I've had a truly blessed life. I've always been surrounded by such amazing people. I've had so many great experiences. I've also learned a lot. The learning wasn't always easy, but I'm thankful for the lessons, nonetheless. Through it all, I'm glad to say that I've grown in Christ.

I don't look at my relationship with Him as a one-time thing that happened the day I asked Him into my heart. It's a daily thing . . . a lifetime thing. I like to call it an "eternal love affair." It's a daily walk with Him. In fact, it's a forever walk. I will love and serve Him forever. Yes, I will follow Christ . . . FOREVER!

Clay Crosse [CHRISTIAN ARTIST]

Out of My Comfort Zone

The police want me to teach the Bible to prostitutes? What a shock! A pastor's wife of many years, I was more at home at a covered dish luncheon than in a motel room in a questionable part of town. This would invade my "comfort zone."

Eventually, I decided I had to trust and follow Christ. After all, these women needed to know the Lord, and I needed to tell them! I began with a covered dish luncheon. Only one "woman of the street" came that first time. I prayed, "Lord, you multiplied the bread to feed the people. Well, we've got the bread . . . so bring on the people!" And He did! The next week, one became two, then two became four, and four became eight. Finally, as many as seventy-eight were fed bread for their physical hunger and then were told about the Bread of Life for their spiritual hunger.

Some women came because of their physical needs, and we fed and clothed them. Some came because we fed and clothed their children. Some came because we told them about Jesus, the One who could fill their greatest need! I wish I could say that all who attended changed their way of living, but that is not so—a few took their own lives. The parents of one young woman even asked me to lead her funeral, which I did. Some women moved on, but many turned their lives around. I am comforted to know that the police no longer have a "sting" operation in that area. When I drive in that area and see none of "my women" on the streets, I stand tall. I'm thankful that my comfort zone got a much-needed adjustment!

Over the years, I have struggled with depression and discouraging circumstances, but I've tried to keep my focus on God instead of on my situations. When I focused on me, God seemed far away, but when I focused on Him, the trials and circumstances seemed small.

While I worked with these women of the streets and learned about their situations, I tried to give them love and hope in Christ. God's faithfulness surely went before me, and I just followed His lead!

Bettye Baker [LAY PERSON IN MINISTRY]

A Mother's Journey

Being a mother has been a spiritual journey for me. It has been a process of inner development and growth.

Early in my life, I looked for a solid foundation. I searched for direction. As a child, my parents would say, "Always know God is watching," or "You can hide from me, but you can't hide from God." As I have grown in wisdom and understanding, I realize that they were trying to teach me a healthy respect for God. It worked, and during struggles later in life, I have said to myself, "God is watching."

When I was younger, I heard that the only way for a family to survive was to raise their children in the church. I believed that, but the struggle to make church a part of my children's lives brought resentment from some of them as well as from my husband, even though he also was raised in the church. I wanted my children to learn how to become a part of a church service. I wanted them to be blessed. I asked God to give our family understanding during this struggle.

When a mother has a child, she is suddenly transformed. With the new arrival, a new spirit awakens within her, and she says, "Dear God, show me and guide my way." Talking to God became part of my daily life as I asked for guidance in nourishing and teaching my children.

Many times, I prayed on my knees, and I am grateful for answered prayer. His timing is always perfect. Never have I asked for a daily portion of God's grace that He did not give me a double portion.

God is first in my life, and I have faith in His wisdom. I am who I am because of His gracious love for me. I will never give up on this journey. My physical body grows weary, yet my spirit and love for Him grows stronger every day. Because of His grace, I am cheerful daily. He directs His thoughts toward me, and they are thoughts of compassion and love.

Deloris Jordan

[MOTHER OF BASKETBALL LEGEND MICHAEL JORDAN]

The twelve of you walked on the earth together

The Father was a brother to you all

The teaching that you heard was the Living Word

The wonders and the miracles you saw

There were times of awesome inspiration

There were times you didn't understand

When He had to go and you felt alone

It must've been so hard to see His plan

I think about the way you carried on

In the face of persecution you stood strong

Jesus said to him, "You shall love the Lord your God

with all your heart,

with all your soul,

and with all your mind."

MATTHEW 22:36

Follow Christ

Compelled to Tell

As a young girl, I accepted Christ into my heart. I did not feel any dramatic sensation, but I knew I was forgiven and I knew that when I died, I would go to heaven.

As a teenager, I was insecure and suffered from low self-esteem. I was born into a family of high achievers, and because of my family name, much was expected of me that I felt I could not deliver. Many times, I was measured by my family name. Not being able to live up to what others thought I should be— what I should look, dress, or act like—made me feel small and inadequate.

I got married young and prayed for children. But children did not come when I thought they would. Now I realize that it was all in God's timing. When the children did come, my husband and I had three children very close together! I was deep into small talk, small toys, small clothes, and small sticky fingers, and although I loved all of this, I knew something else was missing in my life. I was yearning for more.

I suddenly realized that I had lost the focus of my relationship with the Lord. I felt I had let Him down, so I started anew by inviting twelve neighbors over for coffee in hopes of telling them about my walk with the Lord. Only four showed up! But it was a start and a big step for me, a basically shy person.

One afternoon, I felt the Lord calling me into His service. In my spirit, I heard Him say that He would open doors for me that no one would shut. I took this to mean that I was to start a Bible study for women in my city, which I did, and it flourished for twelve years. My focus was back on His Word!

Just as I was led to start the Bible Study, He also made it clear when I was to leave that situation and move on to another calling. I was challenged by God to take up the mantle of an itinerant minister. I wanted to speak to whomever He placed in front of me and tell them of the things He has shown me in His word. I have done this now for twelve years.

Because of His love for me and because I am under His authority, He has . . .

> set me free to—
> commanded me to—
> compelled me to—

"go and tell" others what an impact following Christ has made on my life and what making that same choice can mean to them.

Anne Graham Lotz

[ITINERANT MINISTER AND DAUGHTER OF REVEREND BILLY GRAHAM]

The Story of an Athlete

As a child, I felt driven to succeed. I was bold, willful, aggressive, and strong. Not surprisingly, I was also scared, lonely, confused, and insecure. I wanted to be the best at whatever I was attempting.

I was six years old when my parents divorced. That same year, I also saw my first professional tennis match, and I immediately knew what I wanted to do with my energy. I wanted to become a tennis professional. I begged my mother to allow me to play, and somehow, even though she was a single mom with four kids and very little money, she helped me pursue my dream.

I won the Maureen Connelly Brinker Sportsmanship Award my last year as a junior. I also went to Nationals as an underdog, and I won the event. I became the number-one ranked junior tennis player in the United States and made the cover of *Sports Illustrated*. I turned pro just before my eighteenth birthday.

I won many tournaments, including two Grand Slams. I represented my country three times in the Wightman Cup and played at Wimbledon for twenty-three consecutive years. Injuries took a toll on my career, but I still ended up reaching a career high of No. 17 in singles and No. 10 in doubles.

I accepted Christ at age sixteen. I am extremely fortunate to have become a Christian before I became a world-traveling tennis professional. If I hadn't, my life could have unfolded as tragically as many others' lives have in the high-powered, fast paced, extreme intensity of the professional tennis tour.

Very few people will remember the awards I have received, but in eternity, the things Christ does through me will last forever, especially those things that lead others to Him or enable them to better serve Him.

My role as a new mother and my work with disadvantaged young women fulfills me more than all the trophies I won or could have won. Touching a life for eternity brings me incomparable joy. This is what makes us precious sons and daughters of our Lord and King. "For as many as are led by the Spirit of God, these are sons of God" (Rom. 8:14).

Betsy Nagelsen McCormack

[FORMER PROFESSIONAL TENNIS PLAYER]

Survivors by Grace

I gave my heart to Jesus in our small Midwestern church at the age of eleven. It was an important step for me, almost a rite of passage in our little holiness congregation. What I didn't know then was how it would later save me from total destruction.

As my Dad climbed the corporate ladder in a well-known business machine company, my family moved often. Being the new kid in school certainly had its disadvantages. I was tall, skinny, and shy with lots of freckles. It seemed that I was the last to be chosen for just about everything, which caused my self-esteem to drop. To survive, I stuck close to home and stayed involved at church, where I felt loved and accepted.

Our lives continued in this way with no major problems until my senior year of high school. I was preparing to head off to college, but then my world fell apart. My dad announced that he was leaving us because he wasn't happy at home anymore! He said that it wouldn't affect us kids; he just wasn't able to live with Mom anymore. End of story. No big deal. But he was wrong . . . so very wrong.

I sought refuge by attending a college far from home. There I found a guy, got married, and had the standard two children.

But before long it was ME that was unhappy in MY marriage. Though I had said I would never get a divorce, it appeared to be the only solution to my miserable state.

In the meantime, my two younger brothers had their own problems. One became an unwed father at the age of sixteen and was an alcoholic. The other, after several failed marriages, also developed a heavy cocaine habit. Here we were: three good church kids, in the middle of horrid life circumstances. What had happened to us? At one time, we had all made commitments to follow Christ, no matter what! In the midst of all our pain and struggles, where was He? Did He even care?

He did! He was actually there the whole time, right where we had left Him, waiting for us to turn to Him—and we eventually did. I did not get a divorce and have been happily married to the same wonderful guy for over twenty-six years. My brothers have given their addictions over to the Lord. We are survivors and have lived through some of life's most tragic difficulties, but only by the grace and power of our Lord and Savior, Jesus Christ.

There's no doubt in my mind: For me . . . there's no other way. I will follow Christ.

Debbie Wickwire [PUBLIC RELATIONS PROFESSIONAL]

The Dance of Faith

One of the most "interesting" scenes on any dance floor is the picture of two people who are both trying to lead.

My parents loved Fred Astair and Ginger Rogers movies. Old Fred would glide across the floor, guiding their magnificent footwork. My generation, on the other hand, was the first to dance alone. As a rule, no one leads; people do their own thing to the music and call it "dance." Lots of fun, but lacking the symmetry my parents had when they would roll up the living room rug and become Fred and Ginger, dancing on the moonlit floor after the kids were asleep.

In some ways, my journey as a follower of Christ has been both a beautiful oneness with the Spirit of God and a solo routine that I make up on my own. At times, I tend to ignore the One who constantly wants to teach me to glide above the world I live in and to realize a spiritual dimension that is eternal. In the course of my journey, the decisions I made without considering what God wanted were acts of rebellion that scarred my soul and left me believing the lie of the devil. My life has

been an adventure in which God has proved Himself faithful, even when I wasn't. Today, I find that my past experiences are helpful, especially when I come alongside Christian artists who are facing some of the same decisions I faced.

Pride, talent, personal acumen, and success sometimes fly in the face of letting God lead the dance of my life. During the still morning hours, I hear Him telling me how much He loves me and how temporary all this striving is. He reminds me that I can be used to change the world I live in . . . if I will just let Him lead my steps. When I make that choice with the complete abandon of my will, life becomes a miracle of grace that is filled with inexpressible joy.

George King [ENTREPRENEUR]

Healing the Brokenness

I began my life as unwanted child. In the Korean culture, an unwed girl was not supposed to get pregnant. Giving birth to a girl was even more shameful because a baby girl does not have much value in our culture.

My mother left me at the age of six months with my father, and my father became my world. With him, all things were possible.

When I was twelve, we immigrated to America so that he could have a fresh start. School in America was easy for me. I graduated from high school when I was fifteen. That same year, my father informed me that my mother had died.

My father wanted me to attend college in Korea, but I liked the American life. When I left for college, I wanted to become more "American," so I lightened my hair, wore a different kind of clothing, and I cut my connections with my Korean friends.

By the time I turned twenty-three, my father had five failed marriages and many failed business dealings. In that same year, he shot his business partner and then himself. After his death, I truly felt "orphaned." Before then, I just felt motherless but never an orphan.

I grew up knowing about God but not how He had significance in my life. A girlfriend asked me to her Christian church, where an American evangelist preached. I went to the altar, and I accepted Christ, but without commitment. I ran from God, but He did not let me go. He sent people into my life who were believers and who stood by me faithfully. When another friend invited me to attend her church, I noticed something about her was different. Even in her difficult times, she still had a joyful heart.

God met me in my brokenness. I was a single mother with two sons from a failed marriage, physical pain from a car accident, and years of severe asthma. I felt like I was falling into a black hole with no net to catch me. God slowly started to restore me. He restored me from the broken heart of a little girl.

Seven years ago, I started to seek my mother's relatives. I was looking for answers from my childhood and by God's miracle, I found out my mother was still alive!

God is in the business of miracles. We may stray from Him, but He will never let us go. I now attend a small Korean church close to my house. I went to that church feeling alone and seeking comfort, and before I left, I felt at home. It has been an enriching experience. My sons are settled here, making new friends, and we are healing. I am seeking God's will in my life. As I follow Christ, He is helping me to learn to walk by faith everyday.

Helen Kim-Medina [GRAPHIC DESIGNER]

All I have seen teaches me to trust the Creator

for all I have not seen.

RALPH WALDO EMERSON

My husband Mike, who had spent more time in bars and dancehalls than in church, was explaining to me why he thought Jesus wept. He said, "I think He wept because they just didn't get it. After all He'd done for them—teaching and preaching—His most faithful followers still wanted more from Him to prove His position." Since I'm the one who first told Mike that Jesus was real and not just a mythical character in some ancient book, I've been in awe of his relationship with Christ. It's like introducing an old friend to a special new friend and realizing later that they have a great relationship, whether you're with them or not.

Mike was baptized at twenty-eight, the year after we met. And though we both made a decision to follow Christ, our feet didn't always stay on the path. We had good times and bad times, nearly losing our marriage from the financial stresses that often plague young couples.

One day, a Native American couple stopped in the shop to trade some beadwork for gas and food money. We didn't have any money but invited them to our house for dinner and to spend the night. It turned out they had been told the Antichrist was about to emerge in America, and they were trying to escape the dire predictions of Revelation. Their conversation frightened us terribly. Were they right? Should we go with them? Mike prayed earnestly that night, pleading with God to let us know what to do. Then he saw a blinding white light fill the doorway to the bedroom and a voice simply say, "Just follow me." Mike couldn't believe the voice and light didn't wake me up. That was years ago, but he never forgot the message.

Mike is a top-selling Western artist and sculptor. He has been featured in magazines, newspapers, and on television. He is a founding member of the Cowboy Cartoonist International, and his paintings are collector's items that have been reproduced on greeting cards, mugs, magnets, and tee shirts. He waited for over twenty years for a well-known card company to offer him his own line of cards. In 1999, they did, but that same year, he felt led to donate his time and talents to a children's home in Texas. At the home, he produced an outdoor sculpture park with several gardens and life-size bronze statutes depicting the life of Christ. At that time, Mike felt it was impossible to do both the cards and the sculptures, so he had to turn down the card offer.

When I worry about how we'll get by during this mission we've taken on, I sit in the first sculpture garden dedicated last month, look into Christ's weeping face, and ask for forgiveness. Mike made the best choice, and I'm so proud he had the sense to do it.

Dusti and Mike Scovel

[MIKE IS AN ACCLAIMED WESTERN ARTIST]

I live and love in God's peculiar light.

MICHELANGELO

I don't have to look across the ages

His voice is speaking in my heart today

His Word is like a flame consuming all my shame

His life a shining star to show the way

I Will Follow

To trust God completely requires

the discipline of

surrender.

CHARLES SWINDOLL

The Touch of a Mother

When my father, Samuel Wolgemuth, was a college student, he was called into the ministry. Two years later, he became the senior pastor of Fairview Avenue Brethren in Christ Church in Waynesboro, Pennsylvania. From 1939 to 1952, he served as the only pastor for the seventy-five families in his congregation, and he did it as a full-time volunteer. To keep food on the table, he squeezed enough time into his weekly schedule to sell farm equipment.

Now that I'm grown with children and grandchildren of my own, I realize how incredible this story is, but the real wonder is not primarily the perseverance of my dad but the faithfulness of my mother, Grace Wolgemuth.

The circumstances regarding my own conversion make me smile. I was straight out of the heart of the holiness movement. The Brethren in Christ Church was so conservative that there were no musical instruments in the sanctuary. The women wore plain clothes with no jewelry at all, and the men wore shirts buttoned to the top.

The thing that makes me smile is that God used a motion picture—not a welcomed media form in my conservative family—to touch my heart. Our local civic center was playing "Mr. Texas," the life story of cowboy-singer-turned-Christian Redd Harper. Since it wasn't being shown in a movie theater, our whole family could attend.

At the close of the movie, I sat silently in the back of the auditorium next to my mother. Sensing that the Spirit of God was having His way in her little boy's heart, she asked if I would like to invite Jesus Christ into my life. "Yes, I would," I responded, tears streaming down my face.

Without further direction, I shifted from my chair to my mother's knee, confessed my sin, and thanked God for His mercy. I don't remember the words of my prayer as my mother prompted me, but fifty years later, I am grateful for the power of a repentant heart in the hands of my loving Savior. I'm thankful for God's grace and for parents who led the way.

Robert Wolgemuth [AGENT AND AUTHOR]

I was a teenager in the sixties, but my life was much different from the lives of other girls who were dancing barefoot with flowers in their hair. My mom was suffering from manic depression. I tried to maintain a normal life each day, even while living in the midst of chaos.

One day, my friends and I attended a youth revival. I had given my heart to Jesus when I was seven years old, but that night I wanted to give a "gift" to Jesus. The only thing I had to give was the special gift of art that He had given to me. As I stood at the front of that church, I promised I would do something with His gift that would bring honor and glory to Him.

In 1993, I had a small "fashion jewelry" design business, and I was trying to make a butterfly pin. As I worked, I found myself struggling to make the wings stand up. I finally said, "Lord, if you don't want this to be a butterfly, then what do you want it to be?"

I went back to work, and in no time, an angel pin lay before me. "An angel, Lord? This is August, and people don't want angels except at Christmas!" But the Lord helped me design twelve different angel pins, and I put them for sale on my worktable. By the end of the day, they all had been sold!

Each time someone bought an angel pin, I would tell them that I hadn't made it to honor angels and that it wasn't magic— it was just a piece of metal, shaped like an angel. I created it to remind them that God loved them and was with them at all times.

After Christmas, I thought I would put my angel pins away. But when I came to work, people were waiting to buy these pins to give to their friends who had special needs in their lives. I thought back to that time years ago, when I stood at the front of that church, promising God that I would use my gift to bring glory and honor to Him. THIS WAS IT!

I was intimidated at first, and I was scared. Where will I find people to help me? Where will I get the money? What if no one wants these designs after they've been made? After many nights of worry, my husband said, "Jane, where's your faith?" That shook me back to reality. I had decided to follow Jesus, and if He wanted me to do this project, He would find a way.

I am told that women now wear my angel pins all over the world. This experience taught me to give my concerns to Jesus and to leave them there. If I follow Him, He will guide me every step of the way. He is faithful to His promise.

Jane Davis [JEWELRY DESIGNER]

A Child's Perspective

For the first six years of my life, my heart was prepared, my childlike mind sharpened, and my life molded. Hour after hour, I sat on my maternal grandfather's lap while he read to me out of *Stories from the Bible*. I reveled in the great adventures of David, Samson, Joseph, and Moses. Most of all, I was introduced to Jesus Christ, the One who lived, died, and rose again so that I could know God. A fire was ignited within me then that is still blazing after all these years.

This past Sunday, I watched as a six year old walked the aisle of our church and gave her life to Christ. I was once again reminded of the beauty of childlike faith and the innocence of complete trust. The excitement of new life was so real in her face. I remembered the tent revival in my hometown of Conway, Arkansas, when I first publicly gave my life to follow Christ.

To this day, I can smell the sawdust floor and sense the air of expectancy that beat in my heart. I can picture the big black box that the evangelist used to explain his gospel presentation. We couldn't wait to see what was in that mysterious box. I can still hear the evangelist describing "sin," and then the big

moment came—he opened the box. And out of that box, he pulled one stuffed, black cat after another. Each cat had a piece of paper pinned to it, on which was written a different sin, such as lying, cheating, stealing, and so forth.

As he pulled each toy cat out of the box, my heart became heavier. I felt as if he were talking straight to me! After the last cat was out of the box, the most wonderful thing happened; he explained to everyone how we could be forgiven of our sins by the power and love of Jesus.

That vivid explanation was the greatest thing anyone has ever imparted to me. That truth changed the course of my life and my eternity. When the invitation was given, I was the first one down the aisle. I chose to follow Christ, the One who had given His perfect life for me on the cross. I made a decision, which would set in motion all the paths to come. I'd made a commitment to follow Christ forever.

Jack Graham
[PASTOR OF PRESTONWOOD BAPTIST CHURCH IN TEXAS]

When Ken and I met, we were amazed at the things we had in common. We really understood one another. We finished each other's sentences; we enjoyed the same movies, books, and restaurants; and we shared a common dream—serving God overseas.

As Ken pastored his first church in downtown Chicago, we worked together, learning and waiting for God to show us when to move. We faithfully relied on God but were surprised when our first child became sick. That wasn't supposed to happen! It wasn't part of our plan, yet our first baby was born with a viral infection, which hardened the tissue in her lungs. For months we sat beside her hospital bassinet, listening to the sound of the ventilator filling her lungs with oxygen. Our thoughts were the same: *Our overseas dream is dead.* We now dreamed only of a healthy child.

Ken reacted to the situation with anger and wondered if he should get a different job. We had been willing to go anywhere for God, but watching our child suffer was too much. We did not know what would happen to Hilary, but we discovered that turning away from God was not an option. We chose to stand firm, and two and a half years after she was born, Hilary could breathe on her own.

Driving home from the hospital, Ken and I celebrated, even though we had let go of our dream of overseas missions. We would do God's work in Chicago. Soon we had a second child, and Hilary grew stronger. When Hilary turned seven, the doctors gave her a clean bill of health. Then we had two more children. Soon after, Ken joined the staff of a large church in Tennessee, and God then blessed us with another boy.

In August of 1999, Ken traveled to Kosovo on a short-term mission trip. He helped to rebuild houses destroyed in the war, and his heart was drawn to the people. When he came home, he said, "Melody, what would you think about going to Kosovo?" I knew what he meant. In October, I went to Kosovo and delivered boxes of food to families living in burned out houses. I talked to the people about suffering and hope.

I shared pictures of my children. Many of the women would say, "Five children? You are not American. You are Albanian, like us!"

In the last few months, we've sold our house and most of our belongings. In a few days, we will get on a plane with our five children, ages two through eleven. Taking only what we can fit in our luggage, we are moving to Kosovo. We know a little about suffering, and we know a lot about hope. We have love and Good News to share because we follow Christ. Amid the noise, as we speed down the runway, we will be thinking the same thing—this is the sound of a dream alive!

Melody and Ken Morris [MISSIONARIES TO KOSOVO]

To come to Jesus or to follow him

is to accompany him

into the kingdom.

ALBERT NOLAN

A Life with Christ

I will follow Christ
The sinner cries
I have heard His voice and I will follow Him
With the faith of a child
A child is born again
And he who labors not
Has milk and honey dripping from his chin
He is my hope, He is my life, He meets my every need

I will follow Christ
The child cries
As he stands and bravely tries to walk like other men
When he falls unseen arms surround him
Lifting him up to try again
Each step becomes a step of faith
Each mile a milestone
Slowly he becomes a child
Who stands and stands alone

I will follow Christ
The servant cries
Wraps a towel around himself
And kneels before his friends
Wraps his dreams in garden prayers
And waits for night to end
Cries out "Thy will be done on earth as it is in heaven
In me as in your Son"

I will follow Christ
The old believer cries
And eyes grown dim to this world's light
Look beyond and see a river
A stream no man could cross, save One
But He could walk on water
Then he remembers growing up, falling down
Kneeling in the darkness
I can hear His voice
I will follow Christ

Ray Boltz [CHRISTIAN ARTIST]

I Will Follo

I behold your life and see the man you want me to becom

Living like someone who belongs to the kingdom

That was sealed on Calvary

I will show the world what I believe

Christ

It is not for the flock of sheep to know the pasture

the Shepherd has in mind.

It is for them simply to follow Him.

ELISABETH ELLIOT

The Dallas Hat Lady

For over eighteen years, I found my identity in being a successful realtor, making money, acquiring power and recognition, and being married to a celebrity-type personality.

I also created an identity for myself by wearing hats, fashionable clothes, and dramatic jewelry. This was all for my personal promotion within my business. Even now, you will find me wearing a hat both day and night, and currently, my collection numbers over five hundred hats. I have become known worldwide as "The Hat Lady." A few years ago, I met a couple in Israel while I was riding a camel; they asked me if I was "The Hat Lady from Dallas, Texas."

I've spent many painful years trying to find true significance on this life's journey. My childhood was filled with the trauma of living with alcoholic parents. When I was nine, I was called upon to help raise my six brothers and sisters because our father abandoned us and my mother had to work. I had no direction or leadership, and I learned to survive the best way I could.

I put myself through college and looked for love in the wrong places. I eventually married a flashy man, who was an alcoholic and thirty years older than I was. I longed for a family, and to my delight, we adopted two sons. We were looked upon as the "darling couple" in our social world. After twenty-four years of marriage, I became a widow unexpectedly at age forty-eight. I became a single parent trying to raise my teenage sons, and I soon found out that my husband had left very little insurance money.

In my search for personal significance, making money was at the top of my list. I allowed other things to fall to the side. There was a time when I lost many of the worldly possessions I had worked hard for, things that were very valuable to me. But over the years, survival became important to me as I faced confusion, abuse, cancer, depression, fear, and suicidal thoughts.

I was lost spiritually until I accepted Jesus into my life in 1992. I was baptized at age fifty-two, and I chose to have a covenant relationship with Him and found a new way of life.

Today, what I value most is my relationship in Christ. I use my real estate business as an opportunity to encourage and meet the needs of those that I serve. I also use my gifts of hospitality, creativity, and photography as an encouragement to others.

I have learned to trust in Him and to have a life that reflects His peace and joy. My challenges in life have been worth it because they helped me get to where I am today. My desire is to be a biblical mother, grandmother, and friend and to follow Christ for eternity!

Susanne Forbes Dicker

| WOMEN'S SPEAKER AND REAL ESTATE AGENT |

God's fingers can touch nothing

but to mould it into loveliness.

GEORGE MACDONALD

Searching for Significance

As a young lad growing up, I participated in various sports. Sports were my passion, and I succeeded in a number of them. I wanted to please my father, so I sought his praise through my athletic successes. The encouragement I searched for never came, however, because he was an alcoholic. Needless to say, we did not have a warm, loving relationship. I won numerous high school golf championships and succeeded in college golf events, yet I had a deep longing to be loved and accepted.

While in college, I met a law student who chose to follow Christ. He challenged me to do the same. But I saw no way to accept God's love because I felt like I was a bad person. I was sure I had to earn God's love as I earned everything else. However, I made the decision to accept Christ over thirty-two years ago, and it was the most important decision of my life.

Today, as I teach golf clinics, appear on television, and fulfill speaking engagements, life seems to come easy because God is working through me. What is tough for me is being open with my family. God has blessed me with a tremendous wife

and three beautiful children, and only through Christ am I able to share my emotions with them.

For the past thirty years, I have learned that God will give me the ability to receive love and to give love. As I move from *my* comfort zone, *my* plans, and *my* agendas and into relationships that are in His grip, I can break the ugly patterns of my past. I realize only He can meet my deepest longings for significance. I must allow Him to wrap His arms around me, just as I am.

When my children were young, one of my greatest joys was to hold their hands and tell them how much I loved them. At times, this was hard for me to do. By opening myself up to those who are closest to me, I become vulnerable. It is only through following Christ that I have found the strength and courage to take this step.

My decision to follow Christ is a walk that I take daily. I know that He is the only One who can carry me through and change the patterns of my life that I so greatly desire to have changed.

Wally Armstrong

[GOLF INSTRUCTOR AND FORMER PGA TOUR PLAYER]

In Ministry in Africa

I was born in a village in Rwanda. My parents were animists who worshiped the Supreme Being called Imana through the intermediary of ancestors and the spirits of the dead.

Before I was born, my mother was barren for nine years. Because bareness is believed to be caused by a curse from an ancestor, my mother offered sacrifices to plead for a baby.

When I was born, she named me Musekura, which means "savior." She dedicated me to serve the ancestors as a traditional priest. I was to learn about offering sacrifices, drinks, animal blood, and flesh to the ancestors.

I was fifteen years old when I first saw a white man. He was a missionary. My parents had warned me about white people who might tell me about foreign gods. I was told to never listen because the ancestors would be unhappy, but out of curiosity, most of the village children went to see him.

As we touched him, smelled him, and pinched him (to see if he was real), he would tell us Bible stories. He came every month, and soon a small church was started. When we went to hear him, our parents would beat us. However, I became interested in Jesus, who did not need sacrifices to give people peace.

Two years later, I met the same missionary at a vocational training school, and I gave my life to Christ. Then my life changed dramatically. My family and my village disowned me. They feared that if I visited the village, I would bring suffering and calamity.

After high school, I felt led to serve the Living God. I wanted to go back to my village and tell them and my family about God. My mother could not allow me to come home. My father tried to destroy the ministry and me, but the Lord gave me strength. Eventually, my mother, father, sister, and brother each accepted Christ.

Now I am married with four children. My wife and I are involved in teaching forgiveness and reconciliation to different tribes and groups in Africa. We are training many pastors in Africa who have no biblical or pastoral backgrounds. We want to follow Him in all our ways.

Reverend Cèlestin Musekura [AFRICAN PASTOR]

I will follow Christ
    I will run the race
Fighting the good fight
    Standing on my faith

I will wear the name of Jesus
    I will give Him all my life
As for me no matter what the sacrifice
    I will follow Christ

ow *Christ*

Faith is an active creative force.

J. H. OLDHAM

A Note from the Publisher

How pleased we are to be able to publish *I Will Follow Christ*. We truly believe there is nothing more important in life than following Jesus. We would like to thank our friends, from various walks of life, who shared their hearts and experiences and brought to light the love of Jesus Christ in this book.

When I first heard this wonderful song, I was impressed to develop a book that gave testimony to God's love through the good times as well as the bad times in life. Our prayer and hope is that no matter what your circumstances are . . . you, too, will make the choice to follow Christ.

Marsha and I have had times of joy and times filled with hardships, but God has always been faithful. His timing is perfect, and He is in control of our lives. When I look back, I can see how our decision to follow Christ instead of the world has given us a peace that passes our human understanding. We praise God that today, we have the opportunity to touch lives and change them for His glory.

Jack Countryman